Original title:
Ode to My Monstera

Copyright © 2025 Creative Arts Management OÜ
All rights reserved.

Author: Ryan Sterling
ISBN HARDBACK: 978-1-80581-906-6
ISBN PAPERBACK: 978-1-80581-433-7
ISBN EBOOK: 978-1-80581-906-6

Whispers of the Monstera

In the corner it stands, tall and proud,
Leaves like giants, dancing loud.
It drinks all the water, like it's a beast,
Yet gives me a look, a green leafy feast.

Sunshine on petals, oh what a thrill,
Proudly it boasts of its glorious chill.
Tangled and twisted, a wild hairdo,
I guess we are both a bit askew!

When I beam at growth, it fluffs up with glee,
As if it's saying, "Look at me, I'm free!"
Fingers trace veins, this plant is a tease,
A green little trickster, with charm that won't cease.

Oh monster of mine, with your leafy embrace,
You're my indoor buddy, my leafy space ace.
Together we laugh, through the sunshine and shade,
In this plant-powered saga, I'll never trade!

Leaves of Hope

In the corner, green and bright,
A leafy friend, quite a sight.
With leaves like hands, they wave and sway,
I hope they keep the gloom at bay.

They drink my coffee, a thirst so bold,
In their green crowns, stories unfold.
Yet sometimes I trip, what a blunder,
Those sneaky leaves, always up to plunder!

Nature's Soliloquy

What secrets do you hold in green?
A thousand whispers, hardly seen.
You giggle when the breeze comes by,
A plant but sprightly, oh my, oh my!

You dance alone, as if by chance,
In your pot, you lead a prance.
I swear I've seen you wink at me,
A sassy plant, so full of glee!

Dancing Shadows on the Floor

Your shadows twist, a playful tease,
When daylight comes, oh how you please.
The floor's a stage, the sun a fan,
Watch your shadows dance, oh planty man!

I dare not let a guest look down,
For all your quirks, they'd wear a frown.
Spill the secrets of your show,
Or keep them quiet, we both know!

Whispers of the Tropics

In my home, a jungle vibe,
You sit proud, a leafy scribe.
You soak in sun; I pour the tea,
The world outside, let it be free.

A tropical trip in every leaf,
A constant source of comic relief.
You roll your eyes when I forget,
But let's be honest, you're my best pet!

Veins of Life

In corners bright, you soak the rays,
Your leafy dance, a cheeky craze.
With every drink, you stretch and grow,
A party plant, putting on a show.

Each stem's a tale, you twist and twine,
In horticulture, you're the sunshine.
With every sip of water's sweet,
You bring the joy, a green retreat.

The Secrets of Sunlight

You turn your face to catch the glow,
Silent whispers, but you steal the show.
Each sunbeam's like a tasty treat,
A gourmet feast you just can't beat.

With every leaf a secret told,
In the plant kingdom, you're pure gold.
Chasing light like it's a game,
My house is wild; you're to blame!

Lush Embrace

Your tendrils reach with playful glee,
Wrapping around me, can't break free.
In a jungle of living art,
You've claimed your space, you've won my heart.

Each day I find a new surprise,
Your leafy growth, like clever lies.
Schools of bugs may come and go,
You wear them like a badge, you know!

A Leafy Reverie

Oh, what a sight, you stand so tall,
A leafy giant in my small hall.
You sway with grace, a gentle tease,
In this green space, you reign with ease.

When friends stop by, they shake their heads,
'How do you keep her?' they all said.
But little do they really see,
You're just as quirky as could be!

Solace in Each Frond

In the corner of my room, so bold,
A leafy giant, a sight to behold.
Whispers secrets in green delight,
Gives me shade from the morning light.

Waving arms like a quirky friend,
Leaves that beg for a twist and bend.
I swear it dances when I'm away,
Hiding mischief in the light of day.

Sprouts and stabs in a playful way,
Promises to stay, come what may.
Fingers long and a heart so bright,
Can't help but smile at its leafy bite.

With every leaf, it tells a joke,
In the silence, it's just woke.
A therapy plant at its finest,
In this wild green space, I'm the guinness.

Nature's Luscious Elegy

In the jungle of life, quite absurd,
A plant who thinks it's the final word.
With every leaf, it's plotting schemes,
To take over my home, or so it seems.

I water it like a star on stage,
Yet it sulks with a leafy rage.
Too much sun? Too little fun?
It shouts 'Give me bright or I'll be done!'

The sunlit gossip travels fast,
'Watch out for the plant with roots that last!'
A social climber, always unfurled,
My herbaceous buddy is taking the world.

Every frond is a comic strip,
With tales that make my sanity flip.
Oh, green delight in this frolic scene,
Nature's most humorous, you know what I mean?

Serpent of the Soil

Creeping close with a sneaky twist,
My serpent plant does not exist.
A monster in the greenery hue,
With aspirations to outgrow me too.

Each frond like an arm, a playful tease,
Reaching for the cookies, if you please.
Entwining fingers, a wild embrace,
In this plant-plant duel, no one's safe space.

Stealing sunlight, it holds the claim,
As I scurry to say 'what a shame!'
Mortified by its flair for drama,
Yet I can't help but love its karma.

Together we plot in this homey lair,
My leafy monster, it's a wild affair.
With every inch it treks the floor,
I laugh, it's winning this plant war more.

Embracing the Wild

In the chaos of my indoor zoo,
There's a green beast, it's plotting too.
With spikes and smiles, mischief galore,
A wonderful nightmare I can't ignore.

It stretches out, a graceful sweep,
Dreaming of jungles where giants leap.
An explorer in this four-walled realm,
My leafy friend at the helm.

With two pots and a dream to soar,
It tries to open every door.
A clumsy athlete in a pot so wide,
Its love for adventure I cannot abide.

In laughter and light, we tango and twirl,
My comedic plant, in a steady whirl.
With every leaf, I embrace its style,
Forever bound in our quirky aisle.

The Language of Leaves

In the jungle of my room, green fans sway,
Each leaf a whisper, 'I'm here to stay.'
They gossip about light, sunbathing ace,
"More water, please—don't mind my resting face!"

Silently plotting how to steal my chair,
With a twist and a turn, they dance in midair.
If plants could giggle, mine would have a blast,
Making shade and secrets, caught in laughter's cast.

In the Stillness of Growth

In the corner I spy, a plant in the light,
Stretching and yawning, what a silly sight!
Her leaves are my curtains, protecting the scene,
Like a diva deciding what shade is supreme.

"Where's my coffee?" she asks with a sigh,
While leaning all day, she could reach for the sky.
Life's a routine, dance and sway in delight,
With whispers of chlorophyll, it's a leafy night.

To the Rhythm of Roots

Underneath soil, the roots do a jig,
They tickle and twist, dance moves big.
"My pot's too small!" they dramatically cry,
As they plot a takeover, how high can they fly?

"Just one more inch," they poke and prod,
With a flair for mischief, cheering on the odd.
A root rave beneath, a secret parade,
While I watch amused, a lost serenade.

Vibrance in Stillness

My green beast lounges, keeping it cool,
A master of zen, the ultimate school.
With dots of bright green in martial art pose,
Making photosynthesis the star of the show.

"What's that?" she asks, with a sassy flair,
"Just a leaf snack, you wouldn't dare to share!"
With humor in growth, she takes life in stride,
In a world of her own, my leafy pride.

The Tempest of Tendrils

In the corner, a leafy beast,
With tendrils dancing like a feast.
It grabs my socks, it steals my toast,
A pet plant, or a hungry host?

I trim its leaves with timid hands,
But still it plots and makes demands.
With a wink, it grows in style,
Claiming space with leafy guile.

Each morning brings a leafy prank,
My coffee cup, it surely drank.
Yet in its grasp, there lies some cheer,
A verdant jester, always near.

In the Presence of Growth

Among my clutter, it does thrive,
In its pot, it comes alive.
A glorious jungle, wild and wide,
My tiny room, its verdant slide.

At night it whispers leafy jokes,
While I'm asleep, it grows and pokes.
I wake to find a new surprise,
A vine that dances, oh my, my!

It towers tall, but falls a bit,
The funny way it tries to fit.
With every turn, it finds its way,
In the morning sun, come what may.

Roots of Resilience

Down below, the roots are bold,
A twisted tale more fun than told.
They sneak and crawl, a sneaky crew,
Plotting plans for world debut.

Through soil deep, they stretch and reach,
My plant could teach a handy speech.
"Stay grounded, yet reach for the sky,"
It shouts to leaves that wave up high.

So here we are, a quirky crew,
Me, my plant, and its roots too.
We laugh at all the tangled ways,
Life's a dance, in sunny rays.

The Green Symphony

With leaves like flutes, a leafy band,
In my home, they make a stand.
The rhythm grows, a leafy song,
My plant performs all night long.

A serenade of greens and laughs,
It sways along with playful drafts.
While I sip tea, it takes the lead,
In its wild dance, I take heed.

A solo here, a shuffle there,
In every corner, music in air.
With cheerful hums, it spins and twirls,
My plant, the star, in leafy swirls.

Nature's Lush Embrace

In my living space, a green delight,
A plant with leaves, oh so bright!
It drinks my coffee, takes a peek,
A leafy friend, so unique.

Each leaf a hand, waving away,
To brighten up my gloomy day.
With every drip, it seems to cheer,
My plant's the star, let's make that clear!

Caught in the sun, a basking queen,
With a soul of emerald, she's serene.
Roots in her pot, sturdy and bold,
I swear she keeps secrets untold.

I tell her jokes; she never laughs,
But somehow knows my goofy gaffs.
In this green embrace, we share the space,
A growing bond, my leafy ace!

Serenity in Every Frond

My plant polls me for high tea,
Sipping sunshine, oh so spry.
With every breeze, she has her fun,
Practicing yoga, under the sun.

Drooping leaves, a dramatic flair,
As if to say, 'Do you even care?'
But with a wink, she shoots back light,
A glorious sight, morning or night.

I swear she knows what I'm up to,
Dancing 'round, she whispers, 'Boo!'
A comical show, this green diva,
Who keeps me sane, like a true believer.

Each frond a giggle, each leaf a grin,
Oh, the stories my plant could spin!
In tranquility, she's my sprout,
Crazy adventures, she's got clout!

A Symphony of Verdant Essence

In a pot, an orchestra hides,
Leaves waving like passionate guides.
Fiddles squeak and trumpets blow,
A symphony of green to show!

Each strum a joy, each pluck a tease,
Bringing me calm, putting me at ease.
With a bit of sunlight and water too,
This leafy band plays just for you.

A waltz in the wind, it takes a bow,
Leaving me smirking, wondering how.
Harmony thrives from plant to floor,
Just don't ask it for an encore!

With roots that dance, and stems that sway,
My plant's the star of the cabaret.
A verdant zest, a mock serenade,
In every leaf, a laugh is laid!

Leaves That Speak in Silence

In quiet moments, she seems to chat,
Telling tales from her leafy mat.
'Water, sunlight, that's the key!'
But never says a word to me.

Leaves lending shade, a gentle sigh,
They poke fun at the birds that fly.
Each vein a joke, each spot a prank,
A silent humor no one can rank.

With a tilt and twist, she shows her flair,
Pretending to care, yet unaware.
A perfect muse for my nonsense spree,
Leaves that laugh with glorious glee!

How she thrives, with no care at all,
While I babble on, rise or fall.
In our green embrace, the laughter flows,
My playful plant, in perfect repose!

The Touch of Nature

In my living room, a beast does dwell,
With leaves like hands, it casts a spell.
Sometimes it whispers, sometimes it roars,
Engaging in battles with the dust on floors.

It drinks up water like it's on a spree,
I swear it's plotting to take the TV.
Watch out for shadows—it's stealthy and sly,
My leafy friend may soon learn to fly!

Treasures of the Tropic

Each leaf a treasure, glistening bright,
I think I've found the world's best sight.
With veins like paths on a vibrant map,
It plots my journey, puts me in a trap!

When friends arrive, they gasp with delight,
"Did you invite a jungle?!" they say in fright.
But they don't know it snags the pizza too,
When I'm not watching, it gobbles my food!

The Leafy Lullaby

Oh, my green companion, how you sway,
Telling secrets in an odd leafy way.
At night, you croon a leafy melody,
I dream of jungles and wild symphony.

Sometimes I wonder if you're quite alive,
With your silly antics, you nimbly thrive.
From sun-soaked mornings to moonlit nights,
In the heart of chaos, you spark delight!

Embracing the Wilderness

In the corners of my home, chaos unfolds,
With vines that stretch like mischievous bolds.
You dance in the breeze, give a comedic twirl,
My pet plant comedian in a leafy swirl.

As I trip over pots and wrestle the soil,
You grin from your perch, my green friend of toil.
A wild reminder of nature's embrace,
With you in my home, there's never dull space!

Layers of Greenery

In my jungle, it reigns supreme,
A leafy queen with a sunny gleam.
Grew a new leaf, what a delight,
Now I need a ladder for height!

Water spills, oh what a mess!
Dancing roots, I must confess.
Tried to train you, you mischievous sprite,
Now you're the houseplant with all the might.

With your holes and your grand designs,
I thought I'd prune, but how you shine!
Your photosynthesis is top-tier,
But my gardening skills? They disappear!

You're my green child, a glorious sight,
Catching dust like a seasoned knight.
In this battle of care, know your scheme,
I'll win with humor, that's my dream!

Dreaming in Shades of Jade

In your presence, I find pure bliss,
Each leaf a wink, like a friendly kiss.
You stretch your arms, oh so bold,
Me, the gardener, lost in your fold.

A green explosion, my sidekick dear,
With you around, there's nothing to fear.
Friends come over just to see,
How I've turned my home into a tree!

You steal the show, and it's quite the scene,
I pretend to care; you know I'm keen.
Up on the shelf, you wave and sway,
Stealing snacks is your clever play.

Sometimes I wonder as you grow wide,
If you're plotting to take the outside.
But here you stay, in your cozy glade,
My little thief in a leafy parade!

Celestial Petals

Oh, monstrous friend with a leafy crown,
You thrived where others might drown.
With your emerald leaves, you rock my world,
In this plant battalion, you're the swirled.

Every morning, a comedy show,
I spill the water, you steal the glow.
Roots like octopus arms, oh what fun,
In your leafy labyrinth, I'm always on the run.

Your elegance shines, but there's a twist,
You conspire with the dust, how could I resist?
A spa day planned, yet you keep growing,
Like a green comet, forever glowing.

Daydreaming 'bout the sun's warm embrace,
Yet here I am, in this green space.
So keep stealing socks, I'll let it slide,
Life's an adventure in this leafy ride!

Portrait of a Plant

Oh dear friend with your luscious face,
You charm the room, take up space.
In this portrait, you shine and dance,
A true diva, not leaving to chance.

With mishaps aplenty, we make quite a pair,
You reach for the light, and I pull my hair.
Wilting in style, like a dramatic flare,
Each day's a new tale; it's never bare.

Found you a friend, another small pot,
They say you can't see, but trust me, you've caught.
Together we scheme, plotting our fate,
To water the flowers, oh, what a state!

So here's to the chaos, the joys, and the laughs,
In this plant portrait, we'll take the best paths.
Your silly ways bring sunshine and cheer,
In this botanical world, I'm glad you're here!

Resilience in the Urban Canopy

In a world of concrete and steel,
A green gem boasts its zest for life.
With oversized leaves, it can conceal,
All the chaos and urban strife.

Whispering secrets to passing ants,
It sways with flair, a leafy dance.
Even pigeons stop to take a glance,
At the monstera's bold romance.

Rain drips down like a broken tap,
Yet it thrives, no need for a map.
In the city's heart, it takes a nap,
Dreams of vines and nature's clap.

So here's to the plant with a twist,
In a pot it shows its wild insist.
Laughing at rules, it can't be missed,
In the urban jungle, it's blissfully kissed.

The Hidden Stories of Green

Among the shadows, rich tales grow,
Of a monster that steals the show.
With roots like whispers, soft and low,
It hides adventures, oh, what a fro!

Every leaf a page, it pens the plot,
Of cats that climb and pots that rot.
Tales of sunlight, forget-me-nots,
And the occasional squirrel that forgot.

Underneath its tropical crown,
Lies a world that spins round and round.
With cheeky grins, it'll never frown,
The heart of green in a brick-bound town.

So pluck a leaf, whisper a cheer,
To the plant that brings such vibrant cheer.
In the garden of life, let's all draw near,
To its funny tales we hold dear.

In the Shade of Nature's Majesty

In my living room, there stands the king,
With leaves like fans and a surprising zing.
A crown of green, it knows how to swing,
And in its presence, my laughter takes wing.

It throws a shade that's cool and vast,
While sunlight darts like a youthful blast.
A velvet throne where moments last,
With each petal, I escape the fast.

Little critters find refuge below,
In its leafy arms, they come and go.
A gathering of friends, a ticklish show,
In the goodness of green, we steal the glow.

So here's a toast, to the leafy might,
That sprinkles joy and makes wrongs right.
Waving goodbye to mundane sight,
In nature's shadow, we bask in delight.

Echoes of the Emerald Heart

In a room full of chatter and fun,
Lies a leafy giant, second to none.
With every twist, it has just begun,
To spread its magic under the sun.

It tells the jokes that make us laugh,
A comedian in green, it's quite the half.
Leaves like umbrellas, a leafy giraffe,
In the gallery of life, it's our craft.

When the world feels heavy, it stands so tall,
With resilience, it won't let us fall.
Echoes of laughter fill the hall,
Thanks to this plant that welcomes all.

So let's share tales, sip tea or gin,
To the emerald heart, let adventures begin.
In the warmth of its shade, we all win,
With each leafy moment, we dance, we spin.

The Pulse of Plant Life

In my room, a giant leaf,
Snitches on my lack of grief.
It thrives while I just sit and stew,
Thinking of snacks, maybe two.

Water it, I often forget,
Yet it seems not to fret,
With holes like Swiss cheese, what a sight!
Mocking me like it's the star of the night.

It sways and jiggles with every breeze,
A comical dance that just won't cease.
Roots tangled like spaghetti on the floor,
I swear it laughs when I laugh, for sure!

Each time I scrub the floor beneath,
I wonder if it has some teeth.
For a plant with such a funny face,
It lives here and claims our space.

Flora's Reverie

My leafy friend, so bold and loud,
Shouting secrets to the crowd.
Its music sways, a rustling tune,
Inviting me to join the moon.

Caring for it, quite the chore,
Yet it gives me sass and more.
Flaunts its leaves like a peacock proud,
Whispering, 'You're under my shroud!'

Sometimes it stretches for the sun,
Looks like it's just having fun.
Do I water? Do I feed?
Or does it plot a leafy creed?

Next to me, it watches with glee,
A green companion, wild and free.
Sharing laughs with every glance,
Who knew plants could love to dance?

Living with the Green

In my flat, it steals the show,
A leafy legend, on the go.
It grins with gaping, funky holes,
While I sit here counting goals.

Do I talk? Does it listen well?
Sometimes I think I can't quite tell.
We share the room in goofy style,
Living like this just makes me smile.

It basks beneath the brightest light,
Dreams of growing, reaching new height.
With soil and crazy growing woes,
I'm blessed with laughter where it grows.

Messy leaves all over the place,
I trip on greens—I lose my grace.
But through it all, this bond we make,
With silly plans, our roots awake!

Dancing in the Dappled Light

A wild dancer in the day,
Bobbing leaves just want to play.
In the sun, it does a jig,
With twirls that would make anyone gig.

When I forget to give a sip,
It gives a shake, a leafy quip.
With every tilt and golden shine,
I swear it thinks it's so divine.

Oh, the joy in every vine,
It makes my worries seem so fine.
A tangle of green, what a sight,
Together we dance through the night!

Each day's like a plant-filled rave,
I'm the caretaker, but it's brave.
As I twirl with my leafy mate,
Who would guess it's plant-invade?

Flourish Amidst the Concrete

In a pot on my balcony, sits my green friend,
Punching through the pavement, it refuses to bend.
With leaves like a dragon, it sways to the tune,
Who knew plants could party beneath the full moon?

Sipping sunlight like it's trendy champagne,
While I fumble with schedules, it frolics in rain.
Its growth is a marvel, a botanical jest,
I'm just here for water; it's loving the rest!

Quiet Beauty of the Tropics

In my living room jungle, it steals the spotlight,
Dressed in rich green robes, looking ever so bright.
When friends come to visit, they giggle and grin,
They say, 'This plant's a model, it always fits in!'

Sharing space with dust bunnies, and old coffee cups,
It whispers sweet nothings, while I fill it up.
Its charm's in the chaos, a leafy delight,
Who knew 'houseplants' could throw such a party at night?

Tendrils of Serenity

With tendrils like fingers, it reaches for air,
Stretching out wildly, without a single care.
It brushes the ceiling, then sways with the breeze,
A graceful performer, it's hard to believe!

Its leaves are like smiles, catching sunlight just right,
While I scurry about, making sure nothing's tight.
For every small sip, it gives back a spark,
A leafy comedian lighting up the dark!

Nature's Verdant Canvas

A canvas of green, I'm the artist, they say,
Yet my plant does the painting, in its own playful way.
Dancing to rhythms of life all around,
While I stand there laughing, just waiting to sound!

It raises its leaves, like a crown made of cheer,
My plant is the joker, I'm just here for beer.
Together we flourish, in our quirky domain,
Who knew homegrown laughter could come from a strain?

Unfurling Pathways of Life

In the corner it lurks, so sly,
Its leaves like a fan, oh my!
Each new growth a tale it tells,
Of sunlit days and rain-soaked spells.

With a twist and a turn, it thrives,
Finding light while it connives.
Roots seeking joy, no couch potato,
Swinging leaves, a dance like a tornado.

Water me please, it shouts with glee,
Potential's just waiting under the foliage spree.
Inbound vines with hopes so high,
Who knew that green could live so spry?

So here's to you, my leafy friend,
Your antics make dull days bend.
A jester with leaves, sprightly and bold,
In the saga of growth, you're the gold.

The Language of Climbing Leaves

Whispers from the leafy crest,
Creeping up with jest, no rest.
What secrets lie in greenery vast?
Tell me stories of the past!

Climbing high and reaching wide,
Is there a leaf that you can't guide?
Your mode of talk is quite absurd,
Spoken softly, yet never heard.

Oh, how you wrap, with such finesse,
Around the lamp, you do impress.
A twisty spouse to my old chair,
A lush companion beyond compare.

Sing me songs of chlorophyll dreams,
Of sunny mornings and moonlit beams.
In tangled thoughts, we find our pace,
A funny dance in this leafy space.

Growth in Serpentine Grace

Bending low and swaying high,
Each bend is like a sly hi-five.
Chasing light, like a cheeky rogue,
In your presence, there's no fog.

Twisting tendrils, a clever pass,
Bringing laughter like a glass of sass.
Statements made without a sound,
You're the best friend I've ever found.

Oh, the joy, the little quirks,
Every leaf is where the fun lurks.
In wind's soft whisper, oh so funny,
Your green shenanigans are pure honey.

So flaunt those spots and glorious holes,
With leafy antics, capturing souls.
In this wild dance, my friend, embrace,
You're the life's quirk in nature's grace.

Solitude Among the Leafy Arms

In solitude, you stretch and sigh,
Leafy arms that reach for the sky.
Here's your life, a leafy show,
A party for one, or is it two?

With every leaf, a personal space,
In your jungle world, there's no race.
Prickly humor in a calming shade,
A layout of foliage, self-made parade.

You sit so proud, a comic king,
Draped in greenery, doing your thing.
I chuckle at your leafy plight,
Solitary vibes in morning light.

So here's to the laughs, the quirky charms,
The joys of thriving in leafy arms.
You're not alone, my silly muse,
In this green realm, we cannot lose.

Tides of Verdant Grace

In sunlight's glow, my leafy friend,
You stretch and sway, with no end.
Your leaves, they dance, a clumsy show,
A pirate ship, on waves below.

I water you like it's a race,
Yet still you thrive, with such great grace.
You shout, 'More sun!' like a diva queen,
While I just grin, and rub my screen.

Your roots, they sneak like little ninjas,
Searching for snacks, causing some cringes.
I trip and fall, you giggle loud,
Who knew a plant could be so proud?

Yet through the chaos, joy you bring,
In the jungle of home, my leafy king.
With every flirt of your green attire,
You inspire laughter, and never tire.

The Botanical Ballet

Each morning, a sudden pirouette,
You twist and twirl, no sign of fret.
With a sip of water, a grand debut,
My verdant star, it's all about you.

Your leaves are curtains, so bright, so bold,
A theater of green, where tales unfold.
In the spotlight of sunbeams' chase,
You bow and sway, my plant with grace.

I clapped too loud; you took a bow,
Now here we are, a comedy show.
You flaunt your greens like a diva at sea,
What a sight, my leafy jubilee!

The neighbors stare, they think I'm mad,
Talking to plants? Oh, isn't it sad?
But you're my partner, no stage too small,
In our botanical ballet, we have a ball!

Echoes of the Tropics

In my living room, a tropical spree,
With you as my companion, I feel so free.
Your leaves shout secrets from skies above,
In this green jungle, I fall in love.

You whisper rumors of far-off lands,
With every new leaf, adventure expands.
I swear I heard you laugh one night,
When I tripped over your roots in fright!

At dinner parties, you steal the show,
Guests in awe while you steal the glow.
You wave at friends like a charming rogue,
If life is a party, you're the smart toke.

With your oversized leaves, you claim the space,
A tropical echo of vibrant grace.
Each glance I give, you just toss a grin,
In our little world, we always win!

Green Guardian

Oh guardian of my tidy lair,
You watch my antics with knowing stare.
When I dance like nobody's watching,
You cheer me on, my leafy botching!

With your giant leaves as shields of green,
You protect me from messes unseen.
A bouncer for dust, a friend for flair,
In the chaos of life, you're always there.

When friends drop by, they point and gawk,
"Your plant is smarter than your talk!"
Yet you just smile, swaying with ease,
Even the cat knows to drop to his knees.

Together we laugh at the world's fine ways,
With you, dear leaf, I'm always amazed.
As the green guardian of this domestic scene,
Life's perfect chaos, forever serene.

The Gentle Giant

In the corner, a giant sits,
With leaves so big, they can play tricks.
He steals sunlight, my little thief,
Yet brings me joy, beyond belief.

While friends complain, I just chuckle,
For he thinks my home is a jungle.
A little monster, large and green,
The quirkiest plant I've ever seen.

Each leaf, a boat, my dreams they sail,
Navigating stories, oh so frail.
He leans to chat, a sturdy mate,
And guards my room like a housing crate.

With every droop, my heart does race,
As if he's putting on a face.
"Oh dear friend, time to perk up now!"
His shy response, a gentle bow.

Though some may fear his mighty size,
He's just a friend in leafy guise.
In the world of plants, he reigns supreme,
My laughter echoing, like a dream.

Flora's Embrace

In leafy arms, I find a hug,
So cozy, warm, it's just a plug.
He sways with glee when I walk past,
This green delight, my heart's steadfast.

With every twist and turn he makes,
I wonder if he knows, he quakes.
"Hold on tight!" I jokingly shout,
As he bends more, no doubt about!

He wears a crown of dust and cheer,
And whispers secrets for my ear.
A gossiping plant, what a façade,
No judgment here, just a charade!

I tell him dreams, to grow so high,
"Let's reach the clouds, my leafy guy!"
He wriggles close, with leafy glee,
In our world, it's just him and me.

As I water, he gives a wink,
"More sunlight here?" I pause to think.
In this bond, laughter's all around,
With Flora's embrace, joy is found.

Tracing Nature's Patterns

Oh, leafy friend, what patterns you wear,
In greens and stripes, beyond compare.
A fashion model, my envy grows,
With every leaf, your style just glows.

We sketch the wind, in gentle sway,
With whispers of green, we laugh and play.
Your leaf-lettuce dance, a silly move,
Nature's patterns really improve.

In corners of homes, you stand so bright,
A dancing partner, full of light.
"Is it a jungle? Or just a plant?"
His leaves respond with a mischievous chant!

I twirl around, try to mimic grace,
Your leafy charms, I can't replace.
Life's comical art, made with fun,
In this patterned love, we blend as one.

So here's to you, my leafy muse,
With every twist, our hearts amuse.
Your vibrant green, my greatest treasure,
Together we dance, in pure pleasure.

Emerging from Earth

From the earth, what a sight to behold,
A quirky sprout, with stories untold.
He stretches wide, with a big grin,
"Time to grow, let the fun begin!"

With muddy shoes and a cheeky face,
He digs through soil, a slippery race.
"Look at me, I'm a plant on the go!"
In this leafy game, he steals the show.

Each new leaf is a curious prank,
A green balloon in the garden bank.
"Is that a leaf or a baby kite?"
Laughter echoes, oh what a sight!

Above the ground, he finds the sun,
Swaying and dancing, oh what fun!
He plays hide and seek in the light,
And I can't help but giggle with delight.

So here's to the sprout with a playful grin,
Emerging from earth, where fun begins.
With every twist, my heart will yearn,
To watch you grow and brightly burn.

The Garden Guardian

In the corner, green and proud,
A leafy giant, standing loud.
It guards my plants from being sad,
With vibes so cool, it makes me glad.

A sneaky spider shared a joke,
While I tiptoed, nearly choked.
My Monstera giggled, leaf a-flick,
Said, 'Don't worry, I'm never sick!'

With holes that look like ancient art,
It always plays the best part.
When friends arrive, they raise an eye,
My green friend wears a leafy tie!

So here's to all its fun-filled days,
My monster friend in leafy ways.
No creature here can bring me gloom,
With laughter shared, it lights the room.

Where the Green Unfolds

In a jungle of pots, it reigns so free,
With leaves that wave like sails at sea.
Each morning sun brings peeling checks,
As I sip coffee, it plays the vex.

It stretches long, a playful tease,
Catching dust like it's a breeze.
Sipping water's all it craves,
While I stand guard like it's a rave!

'Grow taller!' I cheer, with a wink,
It nods back, as if to think.
A championship plant, it takes the gold,
With jokes in leaves that never grow old.

Together we laugh in leafy delight,
One silly monster, my garden knight.
In this patch of green, joy does unfold,
With stories of growth that never grow old.

A Sanctuary of Splendor

In this room, a kingdom thrives,
With my Monstera, oh how it jives.
A splendor dressed in shades of green,
The life of the party, the garden queen.

It sways with flair to a funky beat,
Every leaf dancing, oh so sweet.
Neighbors complain, 'What's that sound?'
But it's just my plant, joy unbound!

With a gust, a leaf spills the tea,
Whispers of drought or too much spree.
With a twist and turn, it claims the floor,
"The sun is my stage, I want more!"

Nestled in glory, it's hard to flee,
My leafy diva, wild and free.
In this splendor, I find my cheer,
A sanctuary grows with each passing year.

Tendrils of Purpose

With tendrils reaching for the skies,
My Monstera sports its leafy guise.
A sly grin hidden in each bend,
For mischief's what it will defend!

It sprawls with grace, a sight to see,
Claiming corners with wild glee.
"Oh, watch out!" my other plants say,
"My Monstera's here to play!"

Each day it plots, a plan so grand,
To conquer pots across the land.
A mission of fun, it leaves no trace,
Just smiles and laughter in this place.

So let it grow, and let it roam,
In this quirky, plant-filled home.
With tendrils of purpose, it's clear to see,
My Monstera's the boss, bold and free!

Shade of Serenity

In corners where you thrive, oh friend,
Your leafy arms extend, they bend.
You drink my coffee, claim my chair,
Your green presence, a joyful affair.

You catch the light, a dancing prize,
I swear you've got the sharpest eyes.
Whispers of nature with each sigh,
A plant with sass that's living high.

Your stems a jungle, wild and free,
I've forgotten where the rug should be.
With every drip, the pot obeys,
In your plant world, I'm just a phase.

So here's to you, my leafy mate,
You bring the sun, you brighten fate.
Together we laugh, we grow and sway,
Oh, the joy of you, come what may!

Enchanted by the Green

Oh, green magician on my sill,
You perform tricks that give me thrills.
With every sprout a wink you share,
You're the life coach with foliage flair.

You stretch your leaves, a dramatic roll,
In the spotlight, you play the role.
Spinach jokes? Nah, you're the star,
With a pet that's greener than my car!

You've got more vibes than my playlist,
In your shade, can I resist?
A slapstick laugh, a leafy roar,
Did you just grow? Wait, there's more!

Forever my leafy therapist,
In your presence, I can't resist.
Though sneezes come when dust collects,
Your charm has never left me perplexed!

Canopy of Calm

Beneath your branches, I recline,
You're my buddy, green and divine.
With every breeze, you sway and dance,
In this jungle, I take my chance.

You're the Zen master of my den,
With quirky leaves, you laugh again.
You promise shade on sunny days,
While I nap, you serenade.

With roots that scatter, what a sight,
A leafy workout, pure delight.
You've tangled up my likes and chores,
It's just a plant—who needs the scores?

Yet in your charm, I find my peace,
A riddle leaf that gives me ease.
So here's to us, a duo grand,
Life's funny with you, my leafy friend!

Letters of the Leaf

Dear Monstera, you're such a tease,
Your green letters put me at ease.
Every new leaf's a poet's dream,
You spill your secrets with every seam.

You're taking over, so it seems,
A leafy giant in my schemes.
With each new hole, a laugh I share,
Your fashion sense, beyond compare!

Each time I water, it feels like fate,
You grow so big, I contemplate.
What if you wake and make a stand?
You'd rule this place, oh plant so grand!

So here's my note, my planty friend,
With leafy love that won't quite end.
Your letters speak, in leafy prose,
Together we dance, in nature's throes!

Whispers of the Leafy Giant

In the corner, you stand tall,
With leaves that seem to call.
A green giant with a laugh,
I swear you steal my other half.

You sip my coffee, check my mail,
Debating if you want to sail.
I find you in a twirl,
Beneath your tricks, my heart does swirl.

Each morning, you greet with glee,
Whispering secrets of the tree.
I talk to you in a silly voice,
You respond with silence, what's your choice?

Oh Monstera, with your fronds so wide,
In your presence, I cannot hide.
You cheer me up with your broad grin,
With every glance, I just can't win!

Embracing Green Shadows

In shadows cast, you wear a crown,
Wearing greens of every brown.
You sway and dance like it's a game,
While I call you by your funny name.

You make my room a jungle jam,
I found you snacking on a ham.
Your leaves are thick, each one a tower,
Pretending you're the one with power.

I sometimes trip over your feet,
You tease me back with rooty sleet.
Are you the boss? That's hard to tell,
When every heart you've cast a spell.

So let's embrace our leafy fate,
Just you and me, it's never late.
With laughter shared and sunshine bright,
We'll keep this friendship full of light.

The Elegance of Climbing Vines

Oh how you stretch, a graceful climb,
Against the wall, you seek to rhyme.
Your tendrils reach for the ceiling high,
While I just wonder, oh my, oh my!

You scandalize my books at night,
Holding tight, what a silly sight!
Whispers of leaves make quite the scene,
As I sashay past you, feel so diaphanous and keen.

I joke you're plotting world domination,
From this cozy, leafy foundation.
With every sunbeam, you seem to smile,
Planning your takeover all the while.

In the garden of my oddest dreams,
You blend and shift, or so it seems.
To every guest, you're quite the show,
With your antics and height, steal the glow!

In Praise of My Leafy Companion

Oh leafy friend, with colors bold,
You're more than a green pet, true gold!
When loneliness knocks, you make a plan,
I giggle; they don't understand!

With every leaf, a story's spun,
Like gossip shared among the fun.
Your roots are tangled in my heart,
With you beside me, I'm never apart.

You drink my water and break all rules,
The plant with sass, oh how it fools!
At times you act a bit like a clown,
With your antics, I'll never frown.

So here's to you, my leafy mate,
In this green kingdom, we celebrate!
With every laugh and twisty bend,
In you I've found the truest friend.

Heartbeats Beneath the Canopy

In the jungle of my living room,
A plant with style, it's in full bloom.
With leaves like arms, it waves hello,
As if to say, it steals the show.

Photosynthesis? Oh, what a feat!
Turning sunlight into leafy treat.
While I sip my coffee, peaceful and snug,
My monstera plots a green little hug.

Vines that twist and turn with glee,
Claiming the corner like it's royalty.
Sometimes I wonder, what does it see?
Does it judge my dance, or just drink tea?

So here's to you, giant of grace,
You've claimed this little space.
With every new leaf, my heart does race,
In our silly, leafy embrace.

Enchanted by Green Twists

In my home, you strut and sway,
A leafy king, in disarray.
Your style is bold, yet all so chill,
With every twist, you bend my will.

Your potholes gather, a curious sight,
Excuse me, did I water you last night?
You sip your drink with such finesse,
While I'm here, a stressed-out mess.

Climbing walls like it's a breeze,
Your leafy antics sure do tease.
You drop a leaf, and I fret and sigh,
But deep down, I know, you're a sly guy.

So here's to laughter, green and bright,
To our leafy love, a silly delight.
In your company, everything's right,
Let's dance together, till fall's first night.

The Glory of Leafy Majesty

Oh mighty plant, with leaves so grand,
In your presence, I feel quite planned.
You catch my eye, a regal sight,
Turning my day from dull to bright.

Your stalks stand tall, like royalty true,
While I fumble for my morning brew.
With every turn, you sway with glee,
Are you practicing yoga, or teasing me?

Sometimes I think, you know my quirk,
With your tight-lipped grin, you go to work.
Photos hopping like my thoughts on spree,
Planting laughter, oh what a spree!

In the evening glow, we share our time,
While I eat my snacks, you pine for lime.
Together we're magic, a savory rhyme,
In this dance of joy, oh how we climb.

Spirit of the Lush Sanctuary

In my personal jungle, you take the crown,
With attitude, you'll never frown.
Your leaves peek out like curious eyes,
While I ponder snacks and goofy cries.

Your presence fills the room with flair,
And yet you don't seem to care.
Just lounging there, all big and spry,
With leafy wisdom—oh my, oh my!

Every morning feels like a cheer,
With you here, there's no room for fear.
Unruly vines and leaves abound,
A quirky spirit, so profound.

So let's embrace this leafy spree,
In our wild, green fantasy.
With laughter shared in this sanctuary,
You and I, plant, we're quite the pair-y.

Nature's Tapestry

In the corner sits a plant, so grand,
Its leaves like fans in a rock band.
With every twist, a green surprise,
I swear I see it roll its eyes.

Water me, it seems to plead,
But I forget its thirsty need.
It shimmies as I scurry past,
A silent protest, unsurpassed.

I talk to it, like it's my mate,
It surely thinks I am first-rate.
But here's the catch, it knows my plight,
I'm merely its comedy highlight.

As sunlight spills, it strikes a pose,
In the living room, it steals the shows.
So here's to you, my leafy friend,
Your quirky charm will never end!

The Spirit of the Greenhouse

Inside the glass, the plant takes flight,
It trips on light, it's quite the sight.
With every gust, it bends and sways,
An elegant dance that brightens days.

Oh, how it stretches for the sun,
Acting like it's having fun.
I swear it winks when I'm not near,
Plotting a future binge on beer.

Sometimes I swear it's plotting schemes,
To take me out, dissolve my dreams.
With roots so deep, it claims its ground,
Warning all who dare come around.

But in our truce, we share a bond,
Its leafy laughter, a joyful respond.
In this greenhouse, laughter's the key,
Just a guy and his plant, wild and free!

Story of a Leaf

Once a leaf, so small and spry,
Dreamed of touching the big blue sky.
It flailed with hope, it couldn't sit,
Till one day it learned to stretch a bit.

It swayed with grace, made new friends,
A cactus here, a fern that bends.
Together they plotted a leafy art,
Dreaming of fame, playing the part.

But oh, the wind had other plans,
Twisting it round, like circus fans.
With every blow, it was a blast,
That little leaf was nothing fast.

Yet still it smiles, with every breeze,
For adventure calls, as it aims to please.
So here's to tales from lofty heights,
From a leaf that knows no fright!

In the Company of Green

In a room filled with shades of green,
My monstera reigns, a leafy queen.
With every sunbeam, it turns and bends,
A diva with no need for friends.

It makes me giggle, the way it grows,
A wild child in a plant-filled show.
Sometimes it droops, looking quite sad,
Guess it's tired of being rad.

We share secrets, plant gossip, too,
Laughing at all that we've been through.
It rolls its leaves like eyes of sass,
In this jungle, we're quite the class.

So here's to us, a duo supreme,
With watering can, we plot and scheme.
In the company of green, we dance,
Living our lives in a leafy trance!

The Gentle Caress of Green

In the corner, you stand so tall,
With leaves so wide, you're the life of the hall.
Not just decor, you're a friend,
Who knows all my secrets, to you I depend.

You drink my coffee, or so I suspect,
Your thirst for my love, I can never reject.
In your pot, you do a little jig,
Oh Monstera, you're the ultimate gig!

When I'm losing my mind, you look serene,
Reminding me of the joys in between.
Your vines, they twist, they turn with glee,
Whispering, "Please, come take a tea!"

So here's to you, my leafy friend,
May our laughter together never end.
In this green kingdom, so lush and true,
I've got the best roommate, and it's definitely you!

Illuminating Spaces with Life's Touch

You brighten rooms with a smile so wide,
With every leaf that sways and glides.
A dance of shadows, a whisk of light,
In my humble abode, you're pure delight.

You mock my fashion, but I don't mind,
In your leafy disguise, style is what you find.
Sometimes, you steal my spotlight, it's true,
But hey, who could resist that charming hue?

With every sip of water, you sigh in bliss,
I dream of a world that looks like this.
Your emerald fingers reach for the sun,
Oh Monstera, together we've just begun!

You're the jester in this plant parade,
In our green kingdom, let's not be afraid.
Here's to the laughter and leafy fun,
With you by my side, life's second to none!

Emerald Dreams

In the quiet night, you stretch and breathe,
Dreaming of jungles, it's hard to believe.
With vines to climb and leaves that flirt,
You're my quirky companion, never a blurt.

As I wake up, you plot your schemes,
Crafting kaleidoscopes of emerald dreams.
I swear I've seen you wiggle with glee,
When I joke about your exotic spree.

Your roots dig deep, but your heart stays free,
Creating a sanctuary, just you and me.
With every new leaf, a laugh on parade,
Who knew a plant could throw such a charade?

So here's to chaos in photosynthesis,
To laughter and life in verdant bliss.
Together we'll thrive, this I guarantee,
With you, dear friend, forever we'll be!

Whispering Leaves

Oh, the stories you tell with each little rustle,
In your leafy embrace, I've learned to hustle.
You're the gossip queen of my cozy space,
With secrets of sunlight all over your face.

You laugh as I trip on your extending vines,
I've planted hopes mixed with coffee dines.
With a wink and a sway, you take the lead,
In our little world, you plant the seed.

From morning's light to evening's shade,
You keep me laughing, our escapades made.
A sage with a twist, my leafy delight,
With you, my dear friend, every day feels right!

So here's to you, my little green muse,
Together in chaos, we can't lose.
As I water you down, and you reach for the skies,
In this silly tale, love never dies!

The Monstera Muse

Oh dear friend with holes so bold,
In sunlight, you shine like gold.
Your leaves are big, your stance is grand,
In my tiny apartment, you take a stand.

With every new leaf that you sprout,
I jump for joy, there's no doubt.
You've got more style than I could flaunt,
You know my secrets, my confidant!

When guests arrive, their jaws drop wide,
'What a jungle!' they say with pride.
I smile and nod, play it so cool,
You're just a plant, not a living jewel!

But secretly, you rule the space,
With your charming, leafy grace.
Oh Monstera, you cheeky delight,
In the green kingdom, you're the highlight!

Secret Keeper of the Flora

In the corner, you sit so sly,
A majestic guardian, oh my!
Every wilt and every droop,
You have secrets, what's your scoop?

With your legs of green and holes galore,
You make my house a leafy store.
Your whispers tell of sun and rain,
In leaf language, it's hard to maintain!

I tell you all of my fears,
You listen closely, shed no tears.
Though some might think you're just a plant,
Your advice is true; you're quite gallant!

So here's to you, my leafy friend,
In sunny days and storms that bend.
Keep my secrets, don't chatter away,
You're the best therapist on a leafy day!

Conversations with the Fern

Next to you, my green delight,
We chat about life both day and night.
You sway and nod, so understanding,
In this green world, you're commanding!

Tell me, dear Fern, what's on your mind?
Is it sunlight or soil that you're trying to find?
With fronds so feathery, you wave hello,
My little buddy in a leafy show.

Sometimes, I wonder what plants do think,
Is it water, or sunlight, or more drinks?
You look so wise with your greens so bright,
Are you plotting my hydration plight?

We laugh together, just you and me,
'Oh, look, a bug, let's have some tea!'
You may be quiet, but I know it's true,
In our green chat, you feel it too!

A Breath of Fresh Green

In my cozy nook, you take a stand,
A bright green breath from the land.
You stretch and yawn in morning light,
What a sight, a pure delight!

When I'm grumpy, you cheer me up,
With every leaf, you're like a pup.
Your holes remind me to just let go,
Embrace the chaos, enjoy the flow!

'Oh, my plant, you wise and tall,
What's the secret to having a ball?'
You respond in silence, oh what a tease,
Yet somehow I'm filled with ease!

So here's a toast to your leafy cheer,
You bring such joy year after year.
A breath of fresh green, that's what you are,
My plant companion, my little star!

The Lounge of the Leafy

In a corner, my friend so grand,
With leaves that twist like a fun band.
Sipping sunlight, a true connoisseur,
Hiding from chores, that's for sure!

Flopping and flailing, she'll sway with glee,
When I play tunes from the old CD.
What a diva, needing her stage,
A leafy queen, in her plant-age!

Mocking my taste in decor, so bold,
"More pots, less mess!" she's often told.
Rolling her leaves with a cheeky grin,
Plotting a takeover, which I can't win!

Water splashes, oh what a show,
So much drama, she'll steal the glow.
In this lounge, the vibe's always right,
With leafy laughter, the world's so bright!

Flora's Odyssey

In the jungle of my living room,
A plant named Flora, defying gloom.
She dreams of climbing, mighty and high,
Imagining she can touch the sky!

Through curtains she peeks, with longing eyes,
Plotting her path, to new highs, oh my!
"Adventure awaits!" she seems to cheer,
While I trip over pots, again, I fear.

Imagining vines in a wild race,
Flora's laughter brings a grin to my face.
"Catch me if you can!" she playfully sings,
While I wonder why I don't have wings!

Each day is a quest, each leaf a tale,
With Flora's antics, I cannot fail.
Together we laugh, explorers we be,
In this leafy life, just her and me!

In Search of the Sun

Chasing rays in a frisky dance,
My dear plant dreams of a sunlit chance.
Bending and stretching, she reaches wide,
With a twist of her leaf, it's quite the ride!

"Just a bit more!" I often hear,
As she tips on her pot with little fear.
Oh, how she fanaticizes paths so bright,
Taking every inch as a glorious flight!

Moving her here, she gives me a glare,
"Not enough sunlight! Is that so rare?"
Rolling her eyes in a leafy fit,
"What do I need to be a sunlit hit?"

Each time I adjust her leafy throne,
She sprawls out like she's suddenly grown.
Together we bask, oh what a scene,
Just a plant and me living the dream!

Fronds and Feelings

In the realm of feelings, my plant's the star,
With fronds so feisty, she travels far.
Whispers of secrets through leaves take flight,
Her thoughts are edible, a veggie delight!

"Why'd you forget to water me today?"
Her sulky pose has such a sway.
With a cheeky leaf, she shows her "hurt,"
Making me question my green thumb's dirt!

We share our burdens, she listens so keen,
In our odd friendship, we giggle and preen.
"Do you think I'm too tall?" she won't let it pass,
With a flair for drama, she'll sass with class!

So here's to the fronds of connection so clear,
With feelings and laughter that all can hear.
In a world of plants, funny antics unfold,
Together we thrive, our stories retold!

The Dance of Green

In the corner, she sways, so spry,
With leaves like umbrellas, reaching for the sky.
Every twist and turn, a botanical jig,
I laugh, she's my jungle's best gig.

Light floods in, she catches a breeze,
Her leaves clap along, with utter ease.
I'm dizzy from chlorophyll cha-cha beats,
Oh, what a delight to share these feats!

When dust bunnies come, she's my trusty knight,
Swooping in with green, so bold and bright.
Alien to spiders, they scurry away,
My leafy friend holds the fort, hooray!

A dance of pots, a nightly routine,
Me and my plant, the strangest scene.
We party 'til sunset, just she and I,
In our leafy realm, let's raise a high five!

A Ritual of Growth

Sprinkled water like magic dust,
She stretches and yawns, as plants often must.
I whisper sweet nothings, she lifts her green head,
Together we plot to conquer this spread.

Each new leaf a trophy, plump and proud,
I cheer like a fan in a raucous crowd.
"Look at me!" she shouts with a vibrant display,
"Watch me outgrow that boring cliché!"

Filling the room with a tropical cheer,
While I trip over pots, blushing with fear.
"Oops, my dear friend, that's just my clumsy flair,"
She shakes it off, unbothered, without a care.

Oh, the rituals of growth we adore,
Complete with chaos and maybe some more.
In laughter, we thrive, in giggles we bloom,
Just me and my monster, together we zoom!

Heart of the Jungle

A jungle in my home, oh what a sight,
With leaves spreading wide, that just feel so right.
Vines twist and turn like a playful dare,
The cat tiptoes, unsure if it's fair.

She's wild, she's free, a green masterpiece,
I hide from the chaos, seeking some peace.
"Why's your plant acting like a rogue?"
Oh dear friend, it's living the vogue!

Sipping my tea, she gazes with glee,
"More sunshine, please!" says the diva with spree.
With roots deep in potting soil, she reigns,
In this heart of the jungle, she's got no chains.

When friends come by, she puts on a show,
"Step back, humans, you're moving too slow!"
In her kingdom of chaos, she thrones supreme,
Oh, this green beast surely fulfills my dream!

Sanctuary in Shadows

In corners of darkness, she stands tall,
Creating a refuge, quite the sprawl.
I tiptoe 'round her, in awe, I confess,
This shadowy queen, oh what a mess!

Leaves drape like curtains, a theatrical play,
As I wander through, in a leafy ballet.
"Dance on, dear plant, don't mind my shoe,"
Accidentally kicking pots out of view!

She giggles at sunlight, too bright to embrace,
In her sanctuary, she's found her place.
An emerald fortress, where joys intertwine,
Who knew a plant could throw such a line?

Sharing secrets in whispers, we plot our mischief,
A duo of resilience, it's bliss, so brief.
"Let's play hide and seek!" I shout in delight,
With my green buddy, every day feels right!

A Love Letter in Chlorophyll

Oh leafed wonder, green delight,
You drink my coffee, sip so bright.
With every sip, my guilt grows strong,
Yet, you're the one who does no wrong.

In shadows deep, you dance with glee,
And steal my heart so effortlessly.
Your roots, my dear, a tangled mess,
Still, I admire your leafy dress.

You flop and swag with such great flair,
A selfie star, but do you care?
With every thorn, I love you more,
You are the plant I can't ignore.

So here's my vow in chlorophyll,
Your leafy hugs I can't fulfill.
For every time you drop that leaf,
I'll just assume it's practical grief.

Lattice of Life

In your leafy realm, I trip and stumble,
Your vines entwined, I'm full of mumble.
You reach for windows, bask in sun,
While I just sit, and blink, and run.

Photosynthesis, your magic game,
A green magician, making me tame.
You giggle softly in the breeze,
While I'm stuck here, begging you please.

Your big bold leaves, a perfect shield,
Yet you demand my time, no yield.
Around your pot, I dance and prance,
My own personal green romance.

But when I forget to give you water,
You gasp and droop, oh dear my daughter!
Yet still you thrive, with cheeky smiles,
A verdant queen, reigning with style.

Under the Canopy

Beneath your shade, I find my peace,
A secret world that will not cease.
Your leaves like umbrellas, wide and grand,
Creating coolness in the land.

With every leaf, a tale unfolds,
The stories that this plant beholds.
I must admit, your growth is bliss,
I watch you flourish, can't resist.

Your air is thick with plush delight,
Each inch you grow, a pure delight.
In every crevice, humor grows,
Jokes in the green, that nobody knows.

Yet here's my truth, dear leafy muse,
You judge my clutter, my fussy blues.
Smile if you will, my friend so terse,
But remember, I pay for this universe.

Radiance in the Room

In sunbeams bright, you soak and shine,
Oh, radiant friend, you sip that wine.
A leafy diva, oh-so-proud,
You dapper heart, so green, so loud.

Your fashion sense, a site to see,
With splashed green tones, it's pure jubilee.
I hear you chuckling as I fuss,
With every blooper, you're a plus.

You invite friends with your grand allure,
While I tell jokes, you're my pure cure.
With every leaf, my spirits rise,
A funny plant beneath dark skies.

So here's a toast to you, my gem,
Though plant parenting may overwhelm.
Let laughter bloom, just like your kind,
A room with you, is peace of mind.

www.ingramcontent.com/pod-product-compliance
Lightning Source LLC
Chambersburg PA
CBHW050306120526
44590CB00016B/2519